MOTHERS

MOTHERS

An Illustrated Treasury of Motherhood

Compiled by Michelle Lovric

COURAGE BOOKS

an imprint of
RUNNING PRESS
Philadelphia, Pennsylvania

Canadian representatives: General Publishing Co., Ltd.,
30 Lesmill Road, Don Mills, Ontario M3B 2T6.

9 8 7 6 5 4 3 2
Digit on the right indicates the number of this printing.

Library of Congress Cataloging-in-Publication
Number 92–55009
ISBN 1–56138–272–8
Cover design by Toby Schmidt
Cover illustration by Victor Gilbert
Interior design by Stephanie Longo
Text edited Melissa Stein
Typography by Richard Conklin

Published by Courage Books, an imprint of
Running Press Book Publishers
125 South Twenty-second Street
Philadelphia, Pennsylvania 19103

The publishers gratefully acknowledge the permission of the
following to reproduce copyrighted material in this book:
P. 22: From "Expectant" by Susan Taylor from *In the Gold of the
Flesh, Poems of Birth and Motherhood,* edited by Rosemary
Palmeira, published by The Women's Press Ltd., London.
Copyright © 1990 Susan Taylor.
P. 23: From "Woman to Child" from *Collected Poems of Judith
Wright,* published by Angus and Robertson, Australia, 1971.
Copyright © 1971 Judith Wright.
P. 26: From *The New Baby Book* by Dr. Howard Chilton,
published by J.B. Fairfax Pty Ltd. Copyright © 1990 J.B. Fairfax
Pty Ltd.
Pp. 31, 43: From *Playing After Dark* by Barbara Lazear Ascher,
published by Doubleday, New York, a division of Bantam
Doubleday Dell Publishing Group, Inc., 1986, and William
Collins, London, 1987. Copyright © 1982, 1983, 1984, 1985,
1986 Barbara Lazear Ascher.
P. 39: From *Manuale per Difendersi dalla Mamma* by Gianni
Monduzzi, published by Arnoldo Mondadori Editore SpA,
Milan. Copyright © 1991 Arnoldo Mondadori Editore SpA.

INTRODUCTION

IN THE BEGINNING, THERE IS AND ALWAYS HAS BEEN A MOTHER. FROM OUR FIRST INDEPENDENT BREATH, WE CARRY HER IMPRINT INSIDE US—JUST AS SHE CARRIED US—FOR ALL OUR LIVES.

AT FIRST, THE MOTHER IS THE CENTER OF THE CHILD'S UNIVERSE, BUT SHE MUST MATURE TO BECOME MERELY A STEADFAST STAR, CONTENT TO BE SURROUNDED AND SOMETIMES EVEN ECLIPSED BY OTHERS. IN REARING A CHILD, A MOTHER CREATES A STRONG, CAPABLE, AND INDEPENDENT PERSON WHO WILL LOVE NOT ONLY HER, BUT OTHERS AS WELL—AND SHE MUST ACCEPT THE ULTIMATE RESPONSIBILITY OF LETTING GO. MOST OF ALL, MOTHERS TEACH THEIR CHILDREN LOVE—HOW TO RECEIVE IT, AND THEN TO GIVE.

FROM THE PHYSICAL SENSATIONS OF PREGNANCY, CHILDBIRTH, AND NURSING, TO THE JOYS AND REWARDS OF SHARING LIFE WITH A CHILD, THIS BOOK LINKS VISUAL IMAGES OF MOTHERHOOD WITH WORDS THAT LYRICALLY CELEBRATE THIS ETERNAL SOURCE OF WONDER.

THE WORLD HAS NO SUCH FLOWER IN

ANY LAND,

AND NO SUCH PEARL IN ANY GULF IN

THE SEA,

AS ANY BABE ON ANY MOTHER'S KNEE.

Algernon Swinburne (1837–1909)
English poet

In the beginning there was my mother.
A shape. A shape and a force, standing
in the light. You could see her energy;
it was visible in the air. Against any
background she stood out....

MARILYN KRYSL
20TH-CENTURY AMERICAN WRITER

Children

are the

anchors

that

hold a

mother

to

life.

SOPHOCLES (495–406 B.C.)
GREEK POET AND DRAMATIST

YOU MAY HAVE TANGIBLE WEALTH UNTOLD,

CASKETS OF JEWELS AND COFFERS OF GOLD.

RICHER THAN I YOU NEVER CAN BE

I HAD A MOTHER WHO READ TO ME.

Strickland Gillilan (1869–1954)
American publicist and verse-writer

Thou straggler into loving arms,

Young climber up of knees,

When I forget thy thousand ways,

Then. life and all shall cease.

MARY LAMB (1764–1847)
ENGLISH WRITER

The

good

mother

says not,

"Will you?"

but

gives.

<small>ENGLISH PROVERB</small>

*M*other, give me the sun.

<small>HENRIK IBSEN (1828–1906)
NORWEGIAN DRAMATIST</small>

SOMETIMES THE STRENGTH OF

MOTHERHOOD IS GREATER THAN

NATURAL LAWS.

Barbara Kingsolver
20th-century American writer

The

mother's

heart

is the

child's

schoolroom.

HENRY WARD BEECHER (1813–1887)
AMERICAN CLERGYMAN AND WRITER

Most mothers are instinctive
philosophers.

HARRIET BEECHER STOWE (1811–1896)
AMERICAN WRITER

...Women know

The way to bring up children (to be just);

They know a simple, merry, tender knack

Of tying sashes, fitting baby shoes,

And stringing pretty words that make no sense,

And kissing full sense into empty words;

Which things are corals to cut life upon,

Although such trifles.

Elizabeth Barrett Browning (1806–1861)
English poet

seventeen

WHO RAN TO HELP ME WHEN I FELL,

AND WOULD SOME PRETTY STORY

   TELL,

OR KISS THE PLACE TO MAKE IT WELL?

MY MOTHER.

Ann Taylor (1783–1866) and Jane Taylor (1783–1824)
English writers

It is the nightly custom of every good mother after her children are asleep to rummage in their minds and put things straight for the next morning, repacking into their proper places the many articles that have wandered during the day. . . .

When you awake in the morning the naughtiness and evil passions with which you went to bed have been folded up very small and placed at the bottom of your mind; and on top, beautifully aired, are spread out your prettier thoughts, ready for you to put on.

J.M. BARRIE (1860–1937)
SCOTTISH WRITER

Your mother loves you like the deuce while you are coming. Wrapped up there under her heart is perhaps the cosiest time in existence. Then she and you are one, companions.

EMILY CARR (1871–1945)
CANADIAN ARTIST

I
begin to
love this
little
creature,
and to
anticipate
his birth
as a
fresh
twist
to a knot,
which I
do not
wish to
untie.

MARY WOLLSTONECRAFT (1759–1797)
ENGLISH WRITER

MY LIFE RESHAPES IN YOUR TINY
  UNFINISHED HANDS . . . .
I SWELL TO THE SIZE OF YOUR
  LIFE . . . .
KEEP ME THIS WAY
AS LONG AS YOU WANT.

Susan Taylor
20th-century English writer

You who were darkness warmed
  my flesh
where out of darkness rose
  the seed.
Then all a world I made in me;
All the world you hear and see
hung upon my dreaming blood.

JUDITH WRIGHT, B. 1915
AUSTRALIAN POET

BEAT UPON MINE, LITTLE HEART,
   BEAT, BEAT!
BEAT UPON MINE! YOU ARE MINE, MY
   SWEET!
ALL MINE FROM YOUR PRETTY BLUE
   EYES TO YOUR FEET.

Alfred, Lord Tennyson (1809–1892)
English poet

A

child

is

fed

with

milk

and

praise.

MARY LAMB (1764–1847)
ENGLISH WRITER

The history of man for the nine months preceding his birth would, probably, be far more interesting and contain events of greater moment than all the three-score and ten years that follow it.

SAMUEL TAYLOR COLERIDGE (1772–1834)
ENGLISH POET

OUR BABIES

ARE OUR IMMORTALITY, RIGHT HERE

AND NOW. THEY ARE ALSO THE BEST

PERSONAL GROWTH EXPERIENCE

AVAILABLE. ANYBODY WHO WANTS TO

TREAD A SPIRITUAL PATHWAY THAT

WILL HOLD UP A MIRROR TO THE

PERSON HE OR SHE TRULY IS, NEED

SEARCH NO FURTHER THAN HAVING A

BABY.

Howard Chilton, b. 1946
English-born Australian doctor and writer

Every baby born into the world is a finer one than the last.

CHARLES DICKENS (1812–1870)
ENGLISH NOVELIST

We
find
delight
in the
beauty
and
happiness
of
children
that
makes
the
heart
too big
for
the body.

RALPH WALDO EMERSON (1803–1882)
AMERICAN WRITER

I KNOW NOT HOW TO PART,

WITH TOLERABLE EASE, FROM THE

LITTLE CREATURE.

Mary Rowlandson (c. 1635–1678)
American pioneer

With her fair white hands she held up the child's face and pressed it to
her mouth and bright cheeks, and kissed it with sheer delight.

JOHANS HADLOUB (c. 1300)
GERMAN POET

ALL THE EARTH, THOUGH IT WERE FULL

OF KIND HEARTS, IS BUT A DESERT PLACE

TO A MOTHER WHEN HER ONLY CHILD IS

ABSENT.

Elizabeth Gaskell (1810–1865)
English novelist

Like being in love with a lover,

being in love with a child colors

things. You aren't to be trusted.

Everything is a bit more than it

seems. Everything seems a bit more

than it is.

BARBARA LAZEAR ASCHER
20TH-CENTURY AMERICAN LAWYER AND WRITER

In the Heavens above,

The angels, whispering to one

another,

Can find, among their burning

terms of love,

None so devotional as that of

'Mother.'

EDGAR ALLAN POE (1809–1849)
AMERICAN WRITER

...the hand that rocks the cradle

Is the hand that rules the world...

WILLIAM ROSS WALLACE (1819–1881)
AMERICAN LAWYER AND VERSE-WRITER

*O*nly

a

mother

knows

a

mother's

fondness.

LADY MARY WORTLEY MONTAGU (1689–1762)
ENGLISH POET AND ESSAYIST

I GOT MORE CHILDREN THAN I CAN RIGHTLY TAKE CARE OF, BUT I AIN'T GOT MORE THAN I CAN LOVE.

Ossie Guffy, b. 1931
American writer

Some are kissing mothers and some are scolding mothers, but it is love just the same, and most mothers kiss and scold together.

PEARL S. BUCK (1892–1973)
AMERICAN WRITER

Everybody's

mother

still

cares.

LILLIAN HELLMAN (1905–1984)
AMERICAN WRITER AND DRAMATIST

THERE NEVER WAS A CHILD SO LOVELY BUT HIS MOTHER WAS GLAD TO GET HIM ASLEEP.

Ralph Waldo Emerson (1803–1882)
American writer

WOMEN DO NOT HAVE TO SACRIFICE

PERSONHOOD IF THEY ARE MOTHERS.

THEY DO NOT HAVE TO SACRIFICE

MOTHERHOOD IN ORDER TO BE

PERSONS.

Elaine Heffer, b. 1926
American doctor and writer

Now, as always, the most automated appliance in a household is the mother.

BEVERLY JONES, B. 1927
AMERICAN WRITER AND FEMINIST

Thus it is that amid maternal

caresses...civilisation strides

purposefully on.

GIANNI MONDUZZI, B. 1946
ITALIAN WRITER

You can do anything with children if you only play with them.

OTTO VON BISMARCK (1815–1898)
GERMAN STATESMAN

Give

a

little

love

to a

child,

and

you

get a

great

deal

back.

JOHN RUSKIN (1819–1900)
ENGLISH ART CRITIC AND WRITER

A MOTHER IS NOT A PERSON TO LEAN

ON, BUT A PERSON TO MAKE LEANING

UNNECESSARY.

Dorothy Canfield Fisher (1879–1958)
American writer

When mamma smiled, beautiful as her face was, it grew incomparably more lovely, and everything around seemed brighter. If in life's sad moments I could but have had a glimpse of that smile I should not have known what sorrow is.

COUNT LEO NIKOLAIEVICH TOLSTOY (1828–1910)
RUSSIAN WRITER

. . . EVERY PARENT BELIEVES THAT

THERE IS MAGIC IN THE WATCHFUL

EYE. AS LONG AS IT SEES IT SAVES.

Barbara Lazear Ascher
20th-century American lawyer and writer

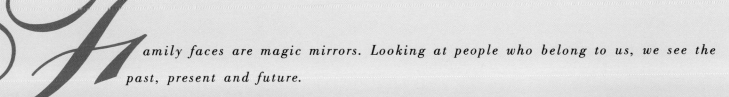

Family faces are magic mirrors. Looking at people who belong to us, we see the past, present and future.

GAIL LUMET BUCKLEY, B. 1937
AMERICAN WRITER

There is nothing more thrilling in this world, I think, than having a child that is yours, and yet is mysteriously a stranger.

AGATHA CHRISTIE (1890–1976)
ENGLISH WRITER

CHILDREN, AY FORSOOTH,

THEY BRING THEIR OWN LOVE WITH

THEM WHEN THEY COME...

Jean Ingelow (1820–1897)
English poet

ILLUSTRATION ACKNOWLEDGMENTS